Frederick Manson Bailey

Plants Reputed Poisonous and Injurious to Stock

Frederick Manson Bailey

Plants Reputed Poisonous and Injurious to Stock

ISBN/EAN: 9783743341906

Manufactured in Europe, USA, Canada, Australia, Japa

Cover: Foto ©Andreas Hilbeck / pixelio.de

Manufactured and distributed by brebook publishing software (www.brebook.com)

Frederick Manson Bailey

Plants Reputed Poisonous and Injurious to Stock

PLANTS

REPUTED POISONOUS AND INJURIOUS TO STOCK.

This paper is an attempt to give in a classified form a brief account of the plants which from time to time have been reputed poisonous or injurious to stock.

It will be observed that several of the plants brought under notice are very unlikely to possess, when eaten with other herbage, properties so poisonous as to be dangerous; but it often happens that these suspected herbs quickly spring up after rain, and being temptingly green and tender—a great contrast, probably, to the surrounding old hard dry grass—animals select this tender bite, which being taken in excess becomes hurtful to them, and is therefore looked upon as poisonous by the stockholder. Others of the supposed poisonous plants are probably only hurtful from their tough fibrous nature, so are rather indigestible than poisonous, and being eaten during times of drought when most of the grass left is also dry, hard, and nearly if not quite destitute of nutriment, the animals die from a want of more succulent food to assist the process of digestion, and not really from poison. Be this, however, as it may, the plants now brought under notice have at one time or other been spoken of as deleterious to stock, and the object sought by the writers is that by thus publishing in a concise form what has been said of the plants, mistakes may be corrected, more reliable information gained, and the stockholder put on his guard against such as are undoubtedly of a dangerous character.

It is thought that a brief popular description of the plants referred to will be more acceptable to the many than a correct botanical description; but those who would prefer the latter will find after each name reference to works where a full botanical description may be consulted and often a plate of the species seen. So far as known the range of each species is given, but doubtless this could be largely extended.

The illustrations will greatly assist in identifying the plants, but should some of these fall short of what could have been desired, it must be borne in mind that in most cases the drawings were made from herbarium specimens, and some of them only fragmentary; so that really much credit is due to the artist (Margaret A. Hope) for the work, taking into consideration the materials she had to work from.

Of several of the plants the illustrations here given are the first published, and, to these, dissectional drawings would have been of additional value, from a botanical point of view; but keeping in mind that this little pamphlet has been prepared for the stockowners and farmers, few of whom have leisure for botanical pursuits, a general representation of a portion of the plant, just sufficient for its identification, has been given.

INDEX.

TRIVIAL NAMES AND PLANTS INCIDENTALLY MENTIONED ARE PRINTED IN ITALICS.

	Page.
Acæna ovina	111
Acæna sanguisorbæ	111
Andropogon intermedius	109
Anthericum bulbosum	103
Anthericum semibarbatum	105
Argemone mexicana	3
Aristida	109, 112
Artimisia sternutatoria	37
Arum	107
Asclepias curassavica	45
Australian Poison-bush	13
Bathurst Burr	33, 35
Bean-tree	29
Beyeria viscosa	77
Black-seed	110
Bladdery Hop-bush	11
Bowen Poison-bush	83
Bulbine bulbosa	103
Bulbine semibarbata	105
Bulli Poison-bush	87
Bunch Spear-grass	111
Buttercups	1
Carumbium populifolium	87
Castanospermum australe	29
Castor Oil Plant	85
Cat's-heads or Caltrops	7
Caustic Creeper	79
Caustic Plant	43
Caustic Vine	43
Centaurea melitensis	111
Centipeda orbicularis	37
var. minuta	37
var. sternutatoria	37
var. lanuginosa	37
Cladosporium herbarum	110
Claoxylon angustifolium	83
Colocasia macrorrhiza	107
Colutea galegifolia	25
Corn Mildew	109
Cnicus lanceolatus	111
Crinum angustifolium	99
Crinum arenarium	99
Crinum asiaticum, var. angustifolium	99
Crinum australasicum, var. arenarium	99
Crinum pedunculatum	101
Croton viscosum	77
Crowfoot	1
Cunjevoi	107
Daphne indica	75
Daphne Mezereum	69
Darling Pea	25

	Page.
Datura Leichhardtii	53
Datura stramonium	54
Desert Poison-bush	13
Devil's Fig of West Indies	3
Dodonæa physocarpa	11
Dogwood Poison-bush of New South Wales	61
Dysphania myriocephala	67
Ellangowan Poison-bush	61
Eremophila maculata	63
Euphorbia Drummondii	79
Euphorbia eremophila	81
Excæcaria Agallocha	89
Excæcaria Dallachyana	91
Fimbristylis diphylla	109
Flinders River Poison-herb	23
Fuchsia Poison-bush	63
Gaoloowurrah	43
Gastrolobium grandiflorum	13, 79
Glœosporium cucurbitarum	110
Goldencups	1
Gompholobium virgatum	13
Gympie	97
Hedge Nettle	65
Helminthosporium Ravenelii	110
Hemarthria compressa	109
Heteropogon contortus	112
Heteropogon insignis	112
Homalanthus populifolius	87
Hoya australis	47
Indigo	25
Indigo-eaters	25
Indigofera australis	19
Ischæmum triticeum	110
Isotropis	13
Kingcups	1
Lactuca scariola	39
Lactuca virosa	39
Lactucarium	39
Laportea moroides	97
Lawrencia spicata	9
Leersia hexandra	109
Lettuce Opium	39
Lettuce, Prickly	39
Lily	101
Lobelia concolor	41
Lobelia pratioides	41
Lotus australis	17
Lucerne fungus	110

	Page.
Madagascar Cotton-bush	45
Mad Apple	55
Maize-rust	109
Martynia fragrans	111
Medic Burr	15
Medicago denticulata	15
Melon fungus	110
Milky Cotton-bush	45
Milky Mangrove	89
Moreton Bay Chestnut	29
Myoporum acuminatum, var. angustifolium	59
Myoporum Dampieri	59
Myoporum deserti	61
Myoporum montanum	59
Myriogyne minuta	37
Native Fuchsia	63
Native Indigo	19, 25
Native Leek	103
Native Onion	103
Native Tobacco	57
Nettle-tree	107
Nicotiana suaveolens	57
var. parviflora	57
var. longiflora	57
Nicotine	57
Nightshade	49
Nooyoora Burr	35
Old Clark	80
Onion	103, 105
Opium	39
Oxylobium	13
Palma Christi	85
Paspalum scrobiculatum	110
Peach-leaf Poison-bush	93
Pimelea hæmatostachya	69
Pimelea pauciflora	71
Pimelea simplex	73
Plagianthus spicatus	9
Poisonous or Strong-scented Lettuce	39
Pratia erecta	41
Prickly Lettuce	39
Prickly Poppy	3
Pterigeron adscendens	31
Puccinia graminis	109
Ranunculus lappaceus	1
Ranunculus rivularis	1
Rattail Grass	110
Redhead	45
Red-rust	109
Rice-grass fungus	109
Ricinus communis	85
River Poison-tree	89
River White Lily	101
Saltern Creek Poison-plant	81
Sarcostemma australe	43
Sarcostemma Brunoniana	43

	Page.
Scotch Thistle of Queensland	111
Scrub Poison-tree	91
Sida rhombifolia	5
Sida retusa	5
Sida-weed	5, 9
Small Burdock	35
Smut	109
Snuff-weed	37
Solanum esuriale	51
Solanum nigrum	49
Sphærella destructiva	110
Sporobolus indicus	110
Stachys arvensis	65
Star Thistle	111
Stenochilus maculatus	63
Stinging-tree	97
Stipa semibarbata	112
Stipa pubescens	112
Stipa setacea	112
Stipa aristiglumus	112
Swainsona galegifolia	25
var. coronillæfolia	25
var. albiflora	25
Swainsona procumbens	26
Swainsona Greyana	27
Swamp Buttercup	1
Swamp Lily	101
Tall Spear-grass	112
Tephrosia purpurea	21
var. brevidens	21
var. rufescens	21
var. longifolia	21
var. sericea	21
Tephrosia rosea	23
Tephrosia cinerea	21
Tephrosia toxicaria	21
Thecaphora globulifera	109
Thorn Apple	53, 55
Thridace	39
Tilletia epiphylla	109
Trema amboinensis	95
Trema aspera	93
Trema cannabina	95
Tribulus cistoides	7
Tribulus terrestris	7
Trichobasis rubigo-vera	109
Uredo linearis	109
Uredo rubigo	109
Ustilago axicola	109
Ustilago carbo	109
Ustilago segetium	109
Wallflower Cotton-bush	45
Wallflower Poison-bush	13, 79
Water Buttercup	1
Waxflower	47
Wikstrœmia indica	75
Xanthium spinosum	33
Xanthium strumarium	33, 35

Ranunculus rivularis

ORDER RANUNCULACEÆ.

RANUNCULUS RIVULARIS,

Banks and Solander in DC. Syst. Veg. i. 270 ; Flora Austr. i. 13 ; F. v. M., Pl. Vict. i. 8.

Swamp or Water Buttercup. In England plants of this genus are often called Crowfoots, Buttercups, Goldencups, and Kingcups.

This plant is frequently met with in Southern Queensland as well as the southern colonies and New Zealand. It has a running stem, which produces tufts of leaves and erect, slightly branched, flowering stalks at nearly each joint. The leaves are produced on long weak stalks, around the summit of which radiate 3 to 7 wedge-shaped leaflets ; these are usually again divided into 3 or even more lobes. The flowers are usually small but numerous and of a bright yellow; the sepals or outer whorl of flower-leaves are small; the petals or inner whorl of flower-leaves are from 5 to 10 in number.

By the sides of creeks and about swamps this plant often produces a large quantity of tempting herbage, and, as species of the same genus are suspected to be poisonous to sheep in Europe, it may be supposed that in times of scarcity of feed mischief may have accrued from sheep feeding on this plant in Queensland. Specimens of the plant have in a few instances been forwarded to the writers, as a suspected poison herb.

The well-known Buttercup so common on our ranges (*Ranunculus lappaceus*, DC.) is one of the reputed poisonous herbs of New South Wales, but we cannot remember any account of its being suspected of deleterious properties in Queensland.

Argemone Mexicana

Order PAPAVERACEÆ.

ARGEMONE MEXICANA,

Linn., Bot. Mag. 243; Synopsis of Queensl. Flora 11; Flora North America i. 61, by Torr. and Gray.

Devil's Fig of the West Indies, and Prickly Poppy of America.

Plant of spreading habit, 2 or 3 feet high, of a light-grey colour. Leaves acutely lobed and spiny, thistle-like. Flower-buds erect, the 3 sepals surmounted by 3 horn-like processes, which arise from their backs. Petals 6, yellow, resembling those of a poppy. Capsule prickly, oblong, containing numerous pitted seeds. Sap of plant yellow coloured.

This thistle-like Mexican plant has become naturalised in a few places in Queensland, but so far as at present known has caused no injury to stock. Really one could hardly suppose stock browsing upon such harsh spiny plants, yet in New South Wales, where it has also become naturalised, it is recorded amongst the plants injurious or poisonous to stock. There are several varieties of this plant, named with regard to the colour of flower.

Sida rhombifolia.

Order MALVACEÆ.

SIDA RHOMBIFOLIA,

Linn., DC. Prod. i. 462; Flora Austr. i. 196.

Sida weed.

This plant, which is more generally known as *Sida retusa*, is a shrubby plant of from 1 to 7 feet in height, with narrow-oval often very blunt leaves from 1 to 3 inches long, toothed, whitish on the underside or in one variety the whole plant whitish from soft short hairs. Flowers small, of a pale-yellow colour, opening about midday, on slender stalks about the length of the leaves, with a joint about the middle. Seeds (carpels) about 10, with usually terminal, erect, conical awns. These carpels have been known to cause the death of young fowls which have eaten them, by producing internal inflammation.

Although detrimental to young fowls, it is in no wise hurtful to stock, except it may be that of occupying space which might be far more profitably covered by grass. Besides being met with in New South Wales, Queensland, and North Australia, it is a common weed of tropical and subtropical countries. In Queensland as well as in India a fibre of excellent quality is obtained from the plant.

Order ZYGOPHYLLEÆ.

TRIBULUS CISTOIDES,

Linn.; DC. Prod. i. 703 ; Flora Austr. i. 288.

Cat's-heads or Caltrops.

A perennial procumbent plant, with densely hairy branches extending to 2 or 3 feet. Leaves abruptly pinnate, opposite, with one of each pair smaller than the other; leaflets 7 or 8 pairs, silky. Flowers yellow, resembling a buttercup, from the axils of the leaves, on a stalk of 1 to 2 inches, succeeded by a roundish, hairy, prickly, dry fruit, composed of 5 carpels, each containing from 2 to 4 seeds ; on the back of each carpel or coccus are 2 or sometimes 4 rather large conical prickles.

This plant enjoys a very wide range, being common in all the warmer parts of Australia, from the Gulf of Carpentaria to the Liverpool Plains in New South Wales; also frequently met with in the West Indies, Tropical America, Pacific Islands; also, but rare, in Tropical Asia and Africa.

From Mr. James Lamond, of Carl Creek, we hear that this plant is said to kill stock if eaten by them on an empty stomach. In Europe, however, of *T. terrestris* (the most common species met with in Australia, and of which *T. cistoides* is probably only a variety) it is said that the fruits hasten the fattening and improve the flavour of fowls fed on them.

ORDER MALVACEÆ.

PLAGIANTHUS SPICATUS,

Benth. in Journ. Linn. Soc. vi. 103 ; Flora Austr. i. 189; figured by Hook.,
Ic. Pl. t. 261 and 262, as *Lawrencia spicata*.

This somewhat harsh shrubby plant, allied to our *Sida* weed, is reported by Dr. R. Schomburgh, of Adelaide, to be injurious to cattle and sheep in South Australia, but only when the plant is seed-bearing. This plant, found in Tasmania and all the other Australian colonies, we may probably sooner or later meet with in this. The injurious effect caused to stock by this and similar herbage is probably only by the prickly, dry, harsh nature of the inflorescence when in seed, which, when eaten in quantity, inflames the mucous membrane of the stomach.

Dodonaea physocarpa

Order SAPINDACEÆ.

DODONÆA PHYSOCARPA,

F. v. M., Fragm. i. 74 ; Flora Austr. i. 484.

Bladdery-fruited Hop-bush.

A tall shrub with the short flowering branches and leaves slightly downy and viscid. The leaves with from 4 to 10 oblong leaflets ¼-inch or more long, sometimes obscurely 2 or 3-toothed, flat, at times thick. Flowers few at the end of the branchlets in a short raceme. Capsule often purplish, large, somewhat inflated, 5 or 6-celled; wings not very broad. Found in North Queensland and North Australia.

Although this has been sent in as a poison bush it is not at all probable that it contains anything injurious to stock. The capsules of several kinds of this genus are used in the bush as a substitute for the common hop in making yeast. Sent as a suspected poison plant from Jericho Creek by Mr. Burrows.

Gastrolobium grandiflorum.

ORDER LEGUMINOSÆ.

GASTROLOBIUM GRANDIFLORUM,

F. v. M., Fragm. iii. 17; Flora Austr. ii. 103.

The Wallflower Poison-bush. This is also known as the Australian Poison-bush and the Desert Poison-bush.

It is a dwarf or at times tall shrub, of a somewhat light-grey colour from being more or less clothed with short soft hairs. Leaves usually opposite, of a harsh dry nature, oblong, and always more or less notched at the top, 1 to 3 inches long. Flowers in the axils of the leaves near the ends of the branchlets, in short often dense panicles, chocolate-coloured, or resembling the flowers of the garden Wallflower; flower nearly 1 inch in diameter. Pods softly hairy, about 1 inch long. This dangerous shrub is met with in North Queensland (inland) and North Australia. Others of the genus constitute the most dangerous poison bushes of Western Australia.

There are no doubts as to the poisonous nature of this bush. So virulent is its poison at certain stages of its growth that working horses and teams of bullocks have to be yarded at night when passing through belts of the plants. Very heavy losses have occurred from it on the road from Cleveland Bay to Hughenden. Drivers and teamsters state that it ceases to be poisonous after the flower appears. On analysis Mr. Staiger failed to discover any active poison, but the analysis was made from dried specimens, and he is of opinion that if freshly-cut specimens were analysed an active poison might be discovered.

Species of the following allied genera—*Isotropis*, *Gompholobium*, and *Oxylobium*—in other parts of Australia, are considered as more or less dangerous poison plants. The Queensland species, however, do not seem to be suspected of deleterious properties, as we cannot remember having received specimens of any as poison plants. This, perhaps, may be because they are not sufficiently abundant in any one locality to cause harm. *Gompholobium virgatum*, Sieb., however, is very abundant on the islands of Moreton Bay, and if really poisonous may have been the cause of the loss of stock reported now and again as occurring on Stradbroke Island (Dunwich).

Order LEGUMINOSÆ.

MEDICAGO DENTICULATA,
Willd.

The Medic Burr.

A prostrate spreading annual, not hairy. Leaves of 3 obovate toothed leaflets. Stipules (the leafy appendages at the base of leaf-stalk) deeply toothed. Flowers small, yellow, axillary, 2 or 3 at the end of a slender stalk about 1 inch long. Pod spirally twisted, forming 2 or 3 loose flat coils, edged with 2 rows of hooked or curved prickles.

A naturalised plant, which during winter and in the early spring months produces a good fodder, yet is a most injurious plant on the sheep station, on account of the prickly burrs deteriorating the value of the wool.

NOTE.—A figure of this plant is given on the title-page of pamphlet.

Lotus Australis

ORDER LEGUMINOSÆ.

LOTUS AUSTRALIS,

Andr., Bot. Rep. t. 624; Flora Austr. ii. 188; Bot. Mag. t. 1365.

A perennial and, in the form most frequently met with in Queensland, of a weak straggling habit, but often in the south forming a dense little bush of 1 or 2 feet high and wide, of a grey colour from the short soft hairs with which the plant is usually clothed. Leaves of 5 leaflets, 3 at the end of the stalk and a lower pair close to the stem, from obovate and about $\frac{1}{2}$-inch long to linear and over 1 inch long. Flowers few or many, forming an umbel at the end of a stalk of several inches in length, usually pink and fragrant, but varying much in colour from white to purplish, with a leaf close under each umbel of flowers. Pods cylindrical, 1 to 1$\frac{1}{2}$ inch long, the seeds separated in the pods by a cellular substance.

This plant is met with in all the Australian colonies, and in the early days of South Australia was considered a good fodder, but of latter years, feed having at times become scarce, it has been looked upon with suspicion, probably unjustly, as we find some species of the genus are recommended to be sown with grass in laying down permanent pastures. Specimens of various forms of this plant have been forwarded to the Chief Inspector of Stock from several parts of Queensland as a poison herb, but there seems little to support the supposition of the plant possessing hurtful properties. Baron Mueller, in Seeman's Journal, 1867, mentioned the reputed deleterious properties of this herb.

Indigofera Australis

ORDER LEGUMINOSÆ.

INDIGOFERA AUSTRALIS,

Willd.; DC. Prod. ii. 226.

Usually an erect shrub of rather loose habit, on the borders of scrubs, attaining the height of 6 or more feet. Leaves of from 9 to 17 oblong obtuse leaflets up to 1 inch long. Flowers reddish, in long or short racemes. Pod nearly straight, 1 to nearly 2 inches long. There are two, if not more, distinct forms in Queensland. In the one the flowers are small, in slender racemes, and the branchlets are not angular as in the common form; this variety is called *gracilis*, and is met with in Southern Queensland, New South Wales, and Victoria. The other forms a more stiff rigid shrub; the numerous rigid leafstalks bearing very small obovate leaflets in distant pairs, with prominent dark-coloured glands at the base. Flowers small, in short racemes.—Queensland, New South Wales, and Victoria.

Baron von Mueller mentions stock having been poisoned by these plants in Victoria.

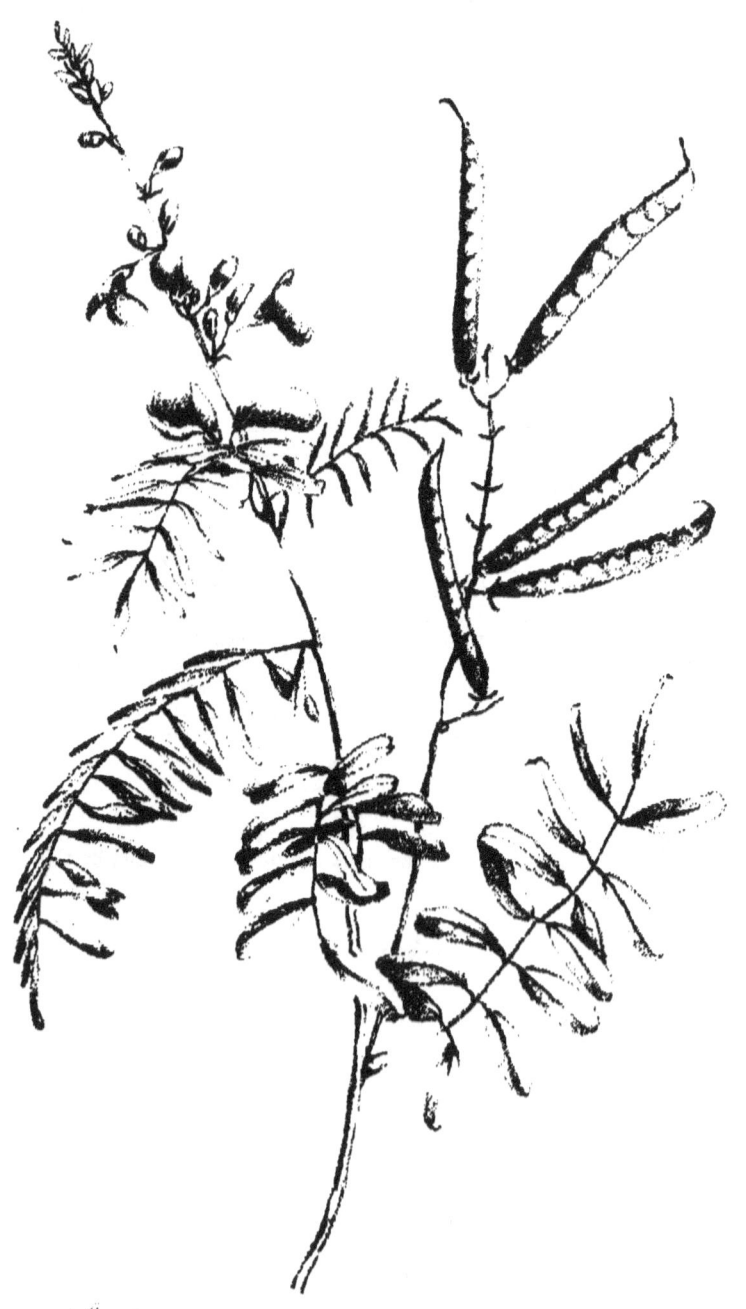

Order LEGUMINOSÆ.

TEPHROSIA PURPUREA,

Pers.; W. and Arn., Prod. 218; Flora Austr. ii. 209.

A straggling plant with or without a coating of close hairs. Leaves composed of from 7 to 11 linear leaflets, the points blunt or with a small recurved point, from $\frac{1}{2}$ to 1 inch long, often silky on the underside; the racemes often short, on the opposite side to the leaf on the branch or at the ends of the branchlets; these usually much longer than the others, bearing distant bunches of 2 to 4 pinkish or purplish flowers under $\frac{1}{2}$-inch in diameter. Pod flat, about $1\frac{1}{2}$ inch long, and more or less curved. There are several forms of this plant in the colony:—

Var. *brevidens*.—An erect shrubby species, hoary, with from 9 to 15 leaflets, and long racemes of flowers; is met with on the north-east coast.

Var. *rufescens*.—A straggling shrub, clothed with red hairs, with about 20 leaflets to a leaf; common on the borders of the Brisbane scrubs and creeks.

Var. *longifolia*.—Of the Gulf country; has long leaflets, often about 2 inches.

Var. *sericea*.—Is clothed with silky hairs; met with on the north-east coast.

Varieties of this species and other species of the genus are known to possess poisonous properties. Some not Australian, as *T. cinerea* and *T. toxicaria*, are used in the West Indies, Fiji Islands, and elsewhere to stupefy fish. For this purpose the stems and leaves are bruised and thrown into the water, when the fish near at hand soon become stupefied.

Tephrosia rosea

ORDER LEGUMINOSÆ.

TEPHROSIA ROSEA,

F. v. M., Flora Austr. ii. 211.

Flinders River Poison-herb.

A densely silky undershrub with leaves of from 5 to 7 oblong often very obtuse leaflets, green on the face but silky on the underside. Flower-racemes long and rigid, bearing small flowers in clusters of 2 or 3 of a pink colour. Pod narrow, densely silky, and much curved. Found in North Queensland and North Australia.

Sent from the Flinders as a poison herb in May, 1885.

Swainsona galegifolia (var. coronillaefolia)

Order LEGUMINOSÆ.

SWAINSONA GALEGIFOLIA,

R. Br. in Ait. Hort. Kew, ed. 2 iii. 327; *Colutea galegifolia*, Sims Bot. Mag.; Flora Austr. ii. 217.

Darling Pea or Indigo.

A perennial or undershrub 1 foot or more high, of a light-grey colour; the leaves composed of from 11 to 21 oblong leaflets, often having their ends notched, from ½ to nearly 1 inch long; the racemes of showy flowers on often long stalks. Flowers deep-red or rosy in one variety (var. *coronillæfolia*), and white in another (var. *albiflora*), large and having at the base of the standard plate-like callosities; the style bearded longitudinally. Pod much inflated and of a membranous substance.

These and some others of the genus are known as "Indigo-plant" in Queensland, where it is common on downs country, also in New South Wales. Although this plant does not contain an irritant poison it has undoubtedly occasioned great losses in stock. Its effect on sheep is well known to stock-owners; they single out from the flock and wander about listlessly, and are known to shepherds as "indigo-eaters." When once a sheep takes to eating this plant it seldom or never fattens, and may be said to be lost to its owner.

The late Mr. Charles Thorn made, in 1873, an experiment with this plant which is deserving of a place here, as showing its effect on sheep. A lamb that had become an "indigo-eater" was placed in a small paddock near the homestead, where it refused to eat grass. Mr. Thorn collected a quantity of the Indigo plant and this it ate greedily, following him all over the paddock and eating it out of his hand.

The Hon. G. King, M.L.C., kindly supplied a bag of the plant to the Chief Inspector of Stock for analysis. Mr. K. T. Staiger experimented on several animals, with the result of showing that it was possessed of very powerful sudorific properties, its effect on frogs, for instance, being to reduce them in a few hours to mere skeletons. Further experiments pointed to the probability of its being a most active poison when administered in a volatile state.

Of the Darling Pea Mr. Wm. Nepean Hutchison says stock readily devour it, and it takes but little to drive them perfectly silly. On one occasion a mob of travelling sheep camped no distance from the town of Taroom. Quantities of the Pea were growing about where the horses were hobbled for the night. The following morning it was noticed how strange the animals appeared. They had been on the road some nine weeks, and were up to this date caught without any trouble, but on this particular occasion it took several of the men to do so. Their eyes were staring out of their heads, and they were prancing against trees and stumps. The second day two out of nine died, and five others had to be left at the camp. When driven they would suddenly stop,

E

turn round and round, and keep throwing up their heads as if they had been hit under the jaw; they would then fall, lie down for a while, and would go through the same agonising performance when they once more attempted to stand. On one station in the course of a few weeks eight head were shot, having injured themselves past all hope of recovery.

There are ten or more other species of the genus *Swainsona* in Queensland, and they likely all possess somewhat similar properties; but the specimens which have usually been forwarded to us as the "Indigo" have been one or other form of *S. galegifolia*. It would seem, however, that in South Australia another species—*S. procumbens*, F. v. M.—is the dreaded plant, and the Adelaide correspondent of the *Brisbane Courier*, in his communication of October 7, 1886, states, "A Bill was carried for the destruction of thistles and *Swainsona procumbens*." A few weeks previous to this a member stated in the House of Assembly, South Australia, that great injury had been done to horses in the south-east by this plant. This species, which is not uncommon in Queensland, is somewhat similar in general appearance to *S. galegifolia*; differing, however, in the absence of callosities on the standard of the flower, and having the keel much incurved and produced into a long, obtuse, spirally twisted beak. The pod is also stalkless and turgid. It is found in South Australia, Victoria, New South Wales, and Queensland.

ORDER LEGUMINOSÆ.

SWAINSONA GREYANA,

Lindl., Bot. Reg. t. 66 ; Flora Austr. ii. 216.

This species, which is suspected of poisonous properties in New South Wales, has been met with in some parts of Queensland, according to Baron Mueller in "Census of Australian Plants," but is not common. It is nearly allied to *S. galegifolia*, differing principally in being of a more robust habit and having the calyx of the flower covered with a cottony down. It ranges throughout South Australia, Victoria, and New South Wales.

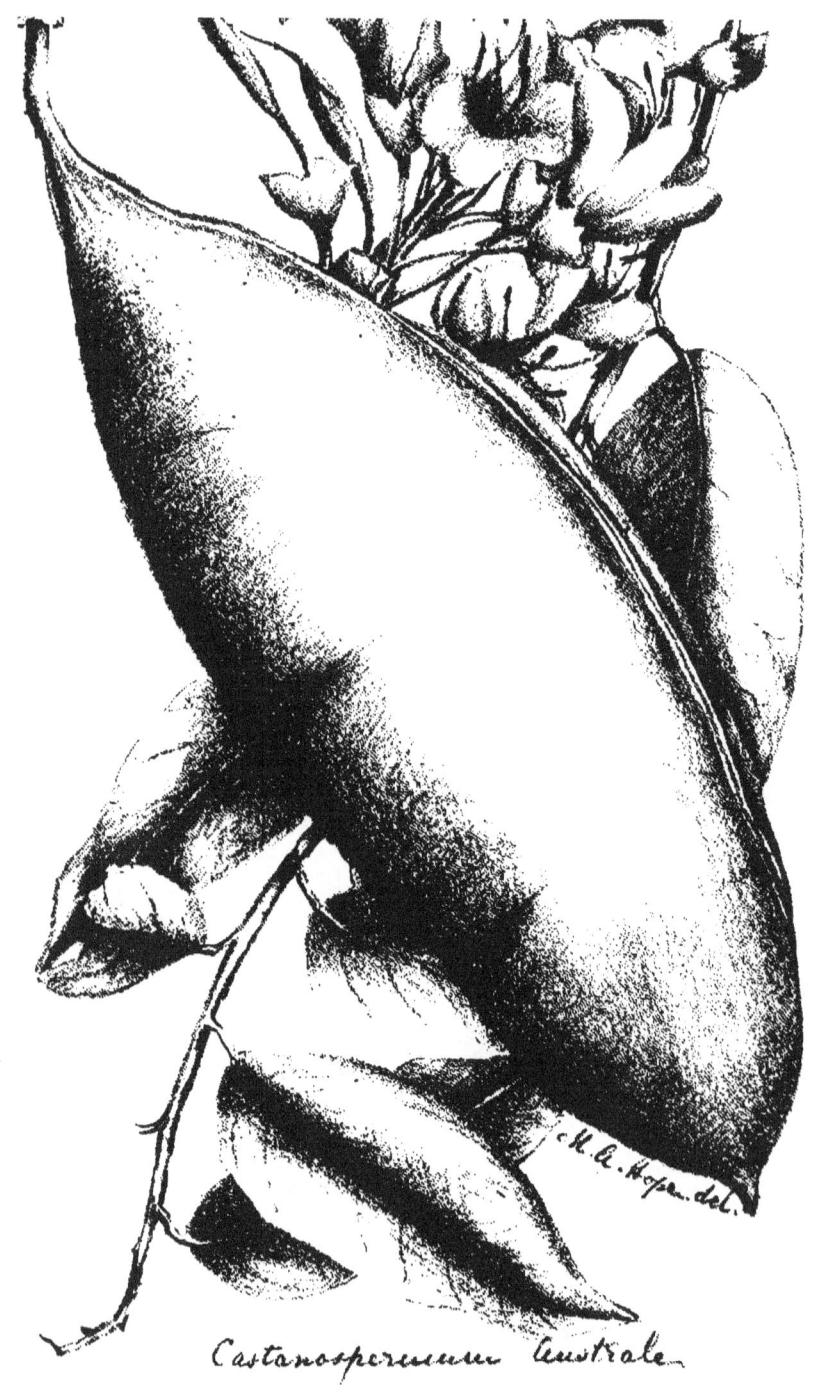

Castanospermum australe

Order LEGUMINOSÆ.

CASTANOSPERMUM AUSTRALE,

A. Cunn. in Hook. Bot. Misc. i. 241 t. 51, 52; Flora Austr. ii. 275.

The Moreton Bay Chestnut or Bean-tree.

This is a well-known and common large tree of the scrubs on the coast side of the ranges. It also is frequently met with along creek-sides, forming a dwarf spreading shady tree; the leaves are large, from 1 to nearly 2 feet long, composed of glossy green leaflets, often over 5 inches long; the flowers are rather large and from a greenish-yellow to a bright red colour, often borne in clusters on the old wood; these are succeeded by large pods of a light-brown colour, frequently over 1 foot long and almost cylindrical, containing closely packed beans resembling chestnuts. Its range is from the north side of New South Wales to the Endeavour River in Queensland.

It is a pretty general belief amongst stock-owners that the beans of this tree are poisonous to stock, and in consequence it has been killed by ringbarking on all purchased land used for pasturage purposes. It is improbable that the beans are poisonous: much more likely the injury to stock is caused by the indigestible nature of the bean. It seems matter for supreme regret that this, one of the handsomest shade trees indigenous to Australia, should be destroyed in such a wholesale manner.

Pterigeron adscendens.

Order COMPOSITÆ.

PTERIGERON ADSCENDENS,

Benth., Flora Austr. iii. 533.

A frequently strong-scented, diffuse, ascending or erect, very much branched herb, with a hard woody base; the leaves linear-oblong, narrowed into a stalk, sometimes with toothed edges. Flower-heads ovoid, rather numerous, about $\frac{1}{4}$-inch or rather more in diameter, the surrounding scales acute and dry, the innermost ones with coloured tips. The pappus or bristles crowning the seed minutely toothed.—Range, North Australia and Northern Queensland (inland).

This herb has been frequently sent from the Gulf country, and also from Ayrshire Downs, as a suspected poison herb.

Xanthium spinosum.

Order COMPOSITÆ.

XANTHIUM SPINOSUM,

Linn.; DC. Prod. v. 523; Flora Austr. iii. 535.

The spiny pest known as "Bathurst Burr."

A shrubby annual plant from 6 inches to 3 feet high, with the stems and underside of leaves whitish, studded with forked sharp spines. Leaves lance-like, 3-cut, the central lobe much longer than the others. The flower-heads are in clusters in the axils of the leaves, the upper flowers male, the lower female, these latter forming in fruit an oblong burr about $\frac{1}{2}$-inch long and covered by hooked prickles.

A wide-spread weed of warm countries, introduced into Australia. From experiments conducted by Dr. Bancroft, this plant, like *X. strumarium*, is at certain stages of its growth poisonous to stock. It is, however, very rarely eaten by them, and the destructive nature of its burrs will suggest to stockowners the desirability of destroying it when found on their runs.

Order COMPOSITÆ.

XANTHIUM STRUMARIUM,
Linn.

In England called "Small Burdock," but usually known in Queensland as the "Noogoora Burr," after the locality where it was first observed to have caused injury to stock.

This annual plant grows to a very large size, often attaining a height of 8 of 10 feet, with wide-spreading branches. The stems, especially in a young state, are mottled with purple; the leaves much resemble those of a Mallow, and are from 2 to 4 inches broad; the burrs are much larger than those of the Bathurst Burr, and the hooked prickles with which they are clothed are coarser.
A widely spread weed of many countries, introduced into Queensland. When young and succulent this plant is decidedly poisonous. About 50 per cent. of a small herd on Noogoora Estate died from its effects. Experiments made by Dr. Bancroft, when the plant was suspected of causing the above heavy loss, proved conclusively its poisonous nature. So far its spread in this colony has been confined to the Moreton district, which is a fortunate circumstance, as its large and tenacious burrs, if allowed to spread to the interior, would cause incalculable injury to wool. Its effect on cattle is to paralyse the heart, induce torpor, and cause death without pain or struggle.

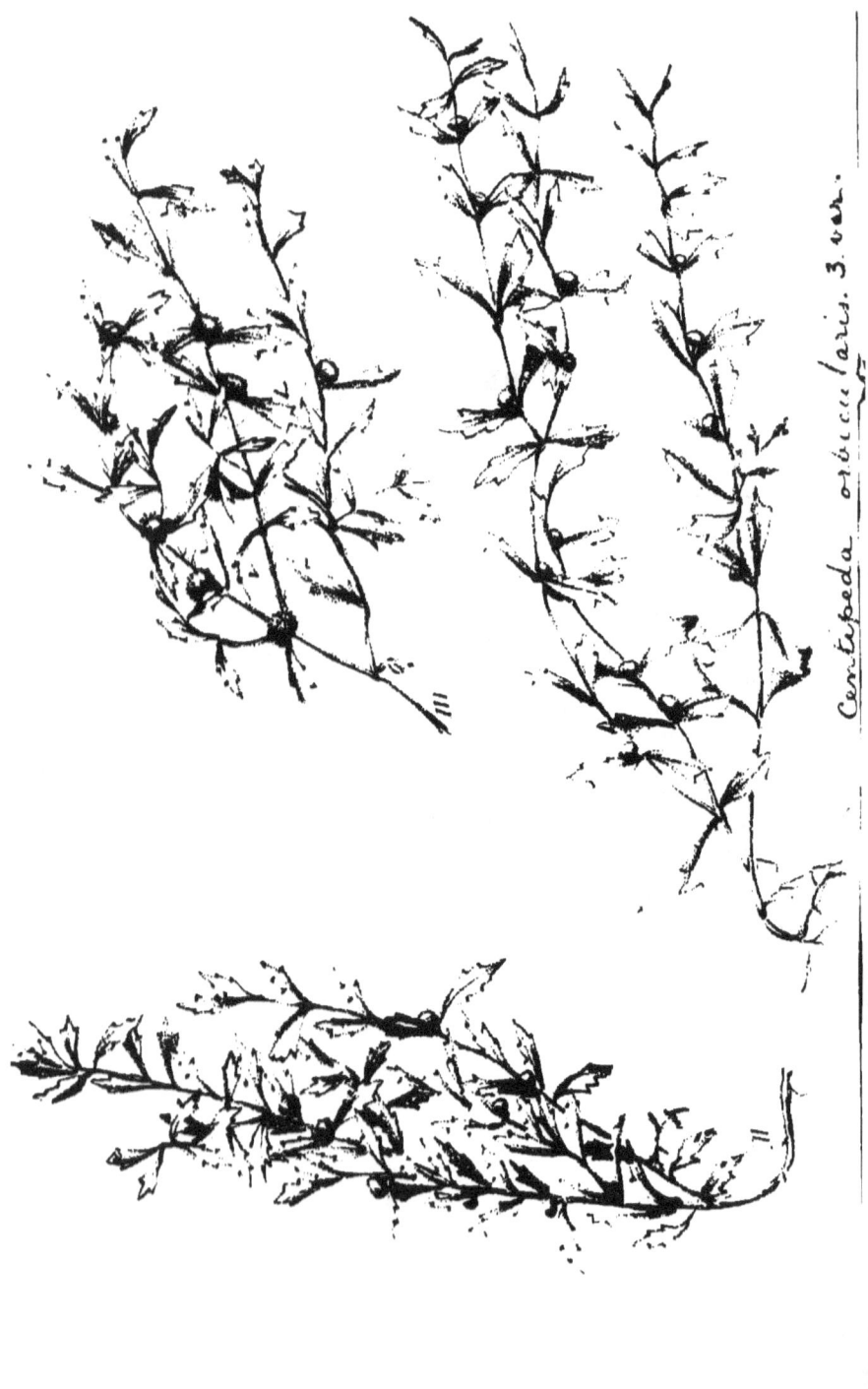

Centipeda orbicularis. 3 var.

Order COMPOSITÆ.

CENTIPEDA ORBICULARIS,

Lour., Miq. Fl. Ned. Ind. ii. 89; *Myriogyne minuta*, Less. in Linnæa vi. 219; Flora Austr. iii. 553.

Snuff-weed.

There are three more or less distinct forms of this plant in Queensland. The one usually to be met with on moist soil in the Brisbane district, and which for convenience will be noticed here as var. *minuta* (fig. i.), is a prostrate, weak plant, nearly glabrous, usually spreading from a few inches to over 1 foot; leaves oblong, about ½-inch long, the lower ones on longish stalks or tapering much towards the base, with a few distant teeth towards the upper end, of a slight pungent scent when bruised; the small heads of insignificant flowers will be found on the opposite side of the stem to the leaf.

Var. *sternutatoria* (fig. ii.). Branches somewhat erect from the procumbent base, and much stiffer than in var. *minuta*, clothed by short rigid hairs, the leaves more pungently toothed. Either green or dry this plant is very pungently scented, and is probably the form called by Roxburgh *Artimisia sternutatoria*, from this fact, and used by him for snuff. In Queensland it is plentiful on the granite soil at Stanthorpe.

Var. *lanuginosa* (fig. iii.). This in habit resembles the last, but is readily recognised by its dense clothing of white silky-woolly hairs. It is the form usually found in the inland districts, in and near the tropics.

A form of this plant was suspected of having poisoned 300 head of stock in the Wagga Wagga district, New South Wales; but, although the plant is so common in Queensland, it has not, so far as we can recollect, been suspected of injurious properties in this colony. A decoction of the herb, however, has been used in the bush as a domestic medicine.

Order COMPOSITÆ.

LACTUCA SCARIOLA,

Linn.; Benth., British Fl. i. 484.

Prickly Lettuce.

An erect stiff annual or biennial from 2 to 5 feet high, of a more or less glaucous green, with short but spreading branches, and quite glabrous except a few stiff bristles or small prickles on the edges or on the midrib of the leaves. Leaves more or less spreading, varying from lanceolate to broadly oblong, either bordered only with small teeth or with a few short lobes or coarse teeth usually curved downwards, or deeply pinnatifid with few narrow lobes; the upper one narrow, more entire, and clasping the stem with pointed auricles. Flower-heads in a more or less leafy panicle, sometimes long and narrow, sometimes more branched and spreading. Involucre 4 or 5 lines long, of a few imbricate bracts, the short broad outer ones passing gradually into the inner long narrow ones. Florets 6 to 10 or 12, of a pale yellow. Achenes much flattened, obovate-oblong, striated, varying in colour from nearly white to nearly black, with a slender beak about the length of the achene.

The name *L. scariola* is often limited to the varieties with more erect leaves, with deeper and narrower lobes; and those with broader leaves, toothed only, and not so glaucous, have been considered as a distinct species, under the name of *L. virosa* (the Poisonous or Strong-scented Lettuce), Bentham, l.c.

We have been informed that this European plant—now a naturalised pest—is sometimes eaten by cattle, on whom it has been observed to have had an injurious effect. It exudes a milky narcotic juice, used medicinally as a mild opium. The drug is called officinally *Thridace*, Lettuce Opium, or *Lactucarium*.

Batis erecta

Order CAMPANULACEÆ.

PRATIA ERECTA,

Gaudich in Freyc. Voy. Bot. 456; Flora Austr. iv. 133; *Lobelia concolor*, R. Br., Prod. 563.

A small erect plant, often producing a cluster of stems from the base, usually about 4 to 6 inches high, but on rich land far exceeding that height. Stems usually well clothed with oblong, toothed, stalkless leaves under 1 inch long, bearing pale, dirty-white, nearly stalkless flowers in their axils, some of which will be observed to be male and others female. The fruit is nearly globular, of about ¼-inch in diameter.

This small plant is met with in all the Australian colonies except, perhaps, Western Australia. Specimens have now and again been sent in of this plant as suspected of poisonous qualities. An allied plant—*Lobelia pratioides*, Benth.—is considered a poison herb in Victoria.

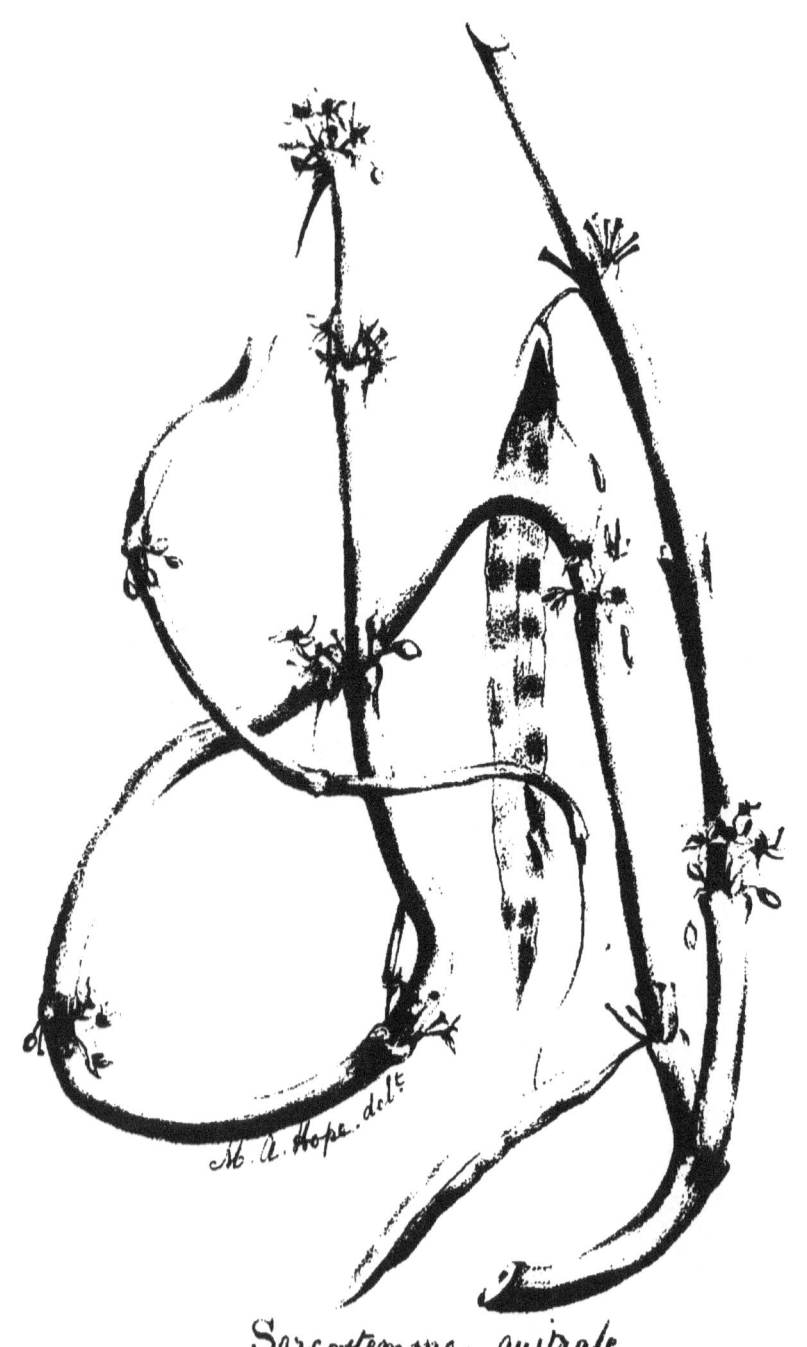

Sarcostemma australe

Order ASCLEPIADEÆ.

SARCOSTEMMA AUSTRALE,

R. Br., Prod. 463; Endl. Iconogr. t. 64; Flora Austr. iv. 328.

Known as "Caustic plant" or "Caustic vine" in Queensland, and "Gaoloowurrah" by the natives at Port Darwin, by whom it is said to be used as a remedy in cases of smallpox.

A leafless, fleshy, climbing, cane-like plant, with a milky juice; the stems round and jointed; the small white flowers are borne in clusters at the joints, and are succeeded by pods (follicles) 1 or 2 inches long, full of seed with a tuft of silky-white hairs at one end. Met with in all the Australian colonies except perhaps Victoria.

Mr. Wm Nepean Hutchison, Inspector of Sheep, Warrego, says that in effect this plant is similar to the Caustic creeper, only far more severe; and that a great number of cattle, chiefly fats, have perished in the Warrego district from eating it.

Mr. Andrew Gordon, when at Vindex Station, writes:—"On the run there is a large waterhole, and around this the plant grows. After a flock of sheep has watered they usually remain for a time around and nibble at plants which they would not touch at other times. It was on occasions like this that sheep ate of this plant, and several deaths occurred in the flock in consequence."

In "Botanical Magazine," 6002, describing *S. Brunoniana*—an Indian species somewhat similar to the Queensland Caustic vine—Sir J. D. Hooker remarks that it abounds in a milky acid juice, and is hence eaten by the natives as a salad, and sucked by travellers to allay thirst, thus forming a remarkable exception to the usually poisonous nature of the Asclepiadeous juices.

Asclepias curassavica.

ORDER ASCLEPIADEÆ.

ASCLEPIAS CURASSAVICA,

Linn.; Dcne. in DC. Prod. viii. 566; Bot. Reg. t. 81; Flora Austr. iv. 326.

Redhead or Milky Cotton-bush, and by some called Madagascar Cotton-bush and Wallflower Cotton-bush.

A West Indian soft-wooded shrub, which has overrun many parts of Queensland; height 2 to 5 feet, with narrow leaves something like Oleander leaves but of a softer nature. Flowers in loose bunches at the end of the branches, of an orange-red and yellow colour. Seed-pods (follicles) smooth, 4 or 5 inches long, tapering much from the base to the point, closely packed with long seeds with a long tuft of silky hairs at one end. A native of the West Indies, but overrunning many tropical regions, and far too abundant in Queensland.

This plant is said to be poisonous to stock, but it is seldom eaten by them except in times of severe drought.

Order ASCLEPIADEÆ.

HOYA AUSTRALIS,

R. Br.; Traill in Trans. Hort. Soc. vii. 28; Flora Austr. iv. 346;
Bot. Mag. 5820.

Waxflower.

A large succulent climber with a milky juice, often met with in scrubs climbing over rocks or tree-trunks, rooting from its joints into the masses formed by other epiphytes, and hanging in long shoots from the branches of the trees. The leaves are usually somewhat oblong with a short point, thick, and from 2 to 5 inches long. Flowers star-like in a dense umbel, white with a more or less pink centre, over $\frac{1}{2}$-inch diameter. Seed-pod (follicle) several inches long, much tapering towards the point, containing closely packed seeds which have at one end a silky tuft of hairs. The plant is found in New South Wales and in most of the rich Queensland scrubs.

A few years ago Mr. C. R. Haly reported having lost a number of sheep from their having eaten this climber while being driven through a scrub in which a quantity of it was growing.

ORDER SOLANACEÆ.

SOLANUM NIGRUM,

Linn., Sp. Pl. 266; Flora Austr. iv. 446.

Small Black Nightshade.

A spreading annual plant with or without a downy clothing of short simple hairs, the angles of the stems often rough with prominent tubercles. Leaves ovate, often with coarse irregular teeth, 1 to 3 inches long. Flowers in little cymes starting from the stem about midway between one leaf and the next, white, star-like, seldom over ¼-inch in diameter, succeeded by usually black berries, but in the more downy plant often greenish; this latter form has often a more prostrate spreading habit, and is considered to possess more poisonous properties. A world-wide weed.

This wide-spread weed has very frequently been brought under notice as poisonous both in this and the other colonies. Some years ago it was reported to have poisoned a number of cattle in Victoria, and those appointed to inquire into the matter gave it as their opinion that the deaths occurred from this cause. The evidence, however, as to the fruit being poisonous is very conflicting. It has been asserted that children have been poisoned by eating the berries raw, but cooked they may be partaken of with impunity. There are two forms of the plant met with in Queensland as before stated, and in all probability the more straggling form with greenish berries is the dangerous kind, and probably, as has been asserted, the plant may possess more or less poisonous properties according to the soil upon which it is grown; thus it may be most dangerous when growing on rich soil, rubbish-heaps, etc., and perhaps quite harmless when growing upon dry poor soil, enjoying the full rays of the sun.

Solanum aviculare

Order SOLANACEÆ.

SOLANUM ESURIALE,

Lindl. in Mitch. Three Exped. ii. 43; Flora Austr. iv. 454.

This plant is usually found about 6 to 12 inches high, with but few branches except those arising from the root-stock; it is covered by a close cottony clothing composed of star-like hairs. The leaves are stalked and somewhat oblong, entire or jaggedly toothed on the edge. Flowers pretty, bluish-purple, nearly 1 inch across, and either singular or 2 or more at the end of the flower-stalk. Berry globular, from $\frac{1}{2}$ to 1 inch in diameter.

This plant is found forming large patches on downs country in Queensland, and is also met with in all the other Australian colonies. We cannot remember its being forwarded to Brisbane as a suspected poisonous herb from any part of Queensland, but it is one of the reputed poison herbs of New South Wales.

Datura Leichhardtii

ORDER SOLANACEÆ.

DATURA LEICHHARDTII,

F. v. M. in Trans. Phil. Soc. Vict. i. 20; Flora Austr. iv. 468.

Native Thorn Apple.

An erect or spreading annual of from 1 to 3 feet high, sparingly downy, with ovate, acute, irregularly toothed or lobed leaves, bearing its whitish flowers in the forks of the branches. Flowers about 2 inches long; corolla with the angles produced into points. Fruit globular, prickly, a little over 1 inch in diameter, reflexed.

This plant is met with in the northern parts of South Australia, North Queensland, and North Australia. From several localities it has been sent to Brisbane as a suspected poison herb.

Datura Stramonium

Order SOLANACEÆ.

DATURA STRAMONIUM,
Linn.

Mad Apple or Thorn Apple.

A soft-wooded heavy-scented annual of 2 or 3 feet in height, with ovate, irregularly toothed, wavy leaves. Flowers white, 3 or more inches long, in the upper forks of the branches. Fruit prickly, over 1 inch in diameter. A wide-spread weed in many parts of the globe.

This plant is decidedly poisonous, although it is questionable whether it is often eaten by stock, except by quiet milkers and working bullocks, which sometimes nibble at it. In 1874 the stomach of a cow, the property of the police magistrate at Toowoomba, that had died from some cause, was forwarded to Mr. K. T. Staiger, then Government analyst, for analysis, and he found a quantity of this plant in the stomach. The cow had been browsing on land about the outskirts of Toowoomba, where this plant was at the time growing in great abundance.

ORDER SOLANACEÆ.

NICOTIANA SUAVEOLENS,

Lehm., Hist. Nicol. 43; Flora Austr. iv. 469.

Native Tobacco.

An erect annual or biennial plant from 1 to 4 feet high, usually clothed with viscid hairs. The lower leaves on long stalks, ovate, often over 1 foot long, the upper ones narrower and usually stalkless, and sometimes clasping the stem with their base. Flower white, fragrant, in one variety (*parviflora*) only about 1 inch long and not spreading much at the mouth; in another variety (*longiflora*), usually met with inland, the flowers are several inches long and expand into an open flower like a Petunia, or Marvel of Peru. Capsule ovate, slightly pointed, and full of small seeds. Met with in one or other form in all the Australian colonies.

There is a general consensus of opinion amongst stockowners that this plant is poisonous to stock. It is credited with causing the deaths of many travelling sheep. Mr. Hutchison instances a case which came under his notice of 300 rams being poisoned by it. The effects upon sheep are drooping head, dull eye, swollen tongue, and, a few hours before death, paralysis of the loins.

Dr. T. L. Bancroft, in a note communicated to the Royal Society of Queensland in January, 1886, has shown that this plant is undoubtedly poisonous, and that this is due to the presence in it of an alkaloid having all the physiological properties of the nicotine of the true Tobacco plant.

Order MYOPORINEÆ.

MYOPORUM ACUMINATUM,

R. Br., Prod.; var. *angustifolium* of the Flora Austr. and Syn. Ql. Fl.; *M. Dampieri*, A. Cunn.; Plate 69 of Baron Mueller's excellent lithographic monograph of the order, lately published.

This variety usually forms a close leafy bush of from 2 to 6 feet in height. The leaves, which are placed alternately on the stem, are about 2 to 3 inches long, of a dark usually glossy green, and taper towards each end from the middle. The stalks are rather long, and the points more elongated than in most other forms of the species. Flowers often rather numerous in each axil, pretty, white, starlike, and usually very hairy inside; these are succeeded by small pinkish or purplish berries, with a fleshy covering to a rather hard stone containing usually 4 one-seeded cells. This shrub enjoys a wide range, being found, according to Baron Mueller's Census of Australia, in all the Australian colonies, including Tasmania. In that work it is given under one of Robert Brown's names, *M. montanum*.

Myoporum deserti.

ORDER **MYOPORINEÆ**.

MYOPORUM DESERTI,

A. Cunn.; Benth. in Hueg. Enum. 78; Flora Austr. v. 5.

Ellangowan Poison-bush. Dogwood Poison-bush in New South Wales.

A close-growing shrub from 1 to 5 feet high, with usually very narrow leaves 1 to 2 inches long, either acute or blunt at the point, and tapering at the base to a very short stalk. Flowers in the axils of the leaves, on rather thick recurved stalks, rather small, and with none or scarcely any hairs in the throat; stamens 5. Fruit ovoid, yellowish-green, of 2 or more cells. This is a common bush in the inland districts of Queensland and all the other Australian colonies.

Like most of the poison or supposed poison plants, these shrubs are seldom eaten except by travelling stock. Mr. A. B. Briggs, of Ellangowan, Darling Downs district, from whom samples have been received, reports that they grow in considerable quantity round a swamp on that run, that they have frequently caused heavy losses in travelling stock there, and that *post-mortem* examination has always disclosed large quantities of these plants in the first stomach.

After the above was written a further packet was received from Mr. Briggs containing specimens in fruit of both these *Myoporums*, and in the letter accompanying the packet he says:—" I am almost certain that these plants are the cause of heavy losses in travelling stock on the Leyburn and Yandilla road. Only last week a mob of sheep belonging to Mr. Gunn, passing that way, lost some hundreds, and on opening them berries and leaves of these plants were found." From this it might be inferred—as was stated some years ago by the late Mr. Jacob Low of *Eremophila maculata*, the Native Fuchsia Poison-bush—that these plants are most dangerous when in fruit.

From letter received while this pamphlet was in the printer's hands, from Mr. Donald Gunn, of Glenlyon, he mentions having lost 500 out of 7,000 sheep travelling past Yandilla by their eating this bush. He also states that nearly every lot of sheep that pass from Dalby to Leyburn, *viâ* Yandilla, lose more or less through this poison-bush.

Eremophila maculata

ORDER MYOPORINEÆ.

EREMOPHILA MACULATA,

F. v. M., Roy. Soc. Tasm. iii. 297; *Stenochilus maculatus*, Ker. in Bot. Reg. t. 647; Flora Austr. v. 29.

Native Fuchsia.

Sometimes tall, but usually a close rigid shrub of 1 to 3 feet; the branches and young foliage more or less hoary; the leaves oblong, about 1 inch long, either acute or blunt at the point, and of a rather dark-green colour; the flower in the axils of the leaves on rather slender stalks, which are usually reflexed but turned up again under the flower; corolla red or variegated with yellow, or quite yellow, about 1 inch long, slightly incurved, 4 upper lobes short, the lowest one narrow, recurved, and separated from the rest to below the middle of the corolla. Fruit ovoid, a 4-seeded nut with a somewhat fleshy covering. This pretty shrub is said to be met with in more or less plenty in each of the Australian colonies.

This plant does not appear to be poisonous to stock accustomed to eat it; but to others, travelling stock particularly, it is considered by Mr. Hutchison, the Stock Inspector of Warrego, to be deadly. Previous to death the stock swell up, eyes protrude, and a greenish discharge flows from the nostrils of sheep. *Post-mortem* showed the stomach to be charged with the plant.

The effects of this plant are always worst after rain. The late Mr. Jacob Low once stated that four of the fruit were sufficient to kill a sheep, and that the plant was therefore most dangerous when in fruit.

Stachys Arvensis

Order LABIATÆ.

STACHYS ARVENSIS,

Linn.; Benth. in DC. Prod. xii. 477; Flora Austr. v. 73.

This little English weed, called the Common Hedge Nettle, has been introduced into the cultivation fields and is now a pest in lucerne paddocks, and especially in badly cultivated lands. It is from a few inches to over 1 foot high, and produces many stems from the base. The whole plant is hairy; the leaves heart-shaped, obtuse and bluntly toothed. Flowers small, pale purple, from 2 to 6 in a whorl forming a loose leafy spike. Calyx of 5 nearly equal teeth. Corolla scarcely exceeding the calyx, the upper lip erect, entire, the lip spreading and of 3 lobes. Stamens 4, in pairs, ascending under the upper lip.

It must strike one as rather remarkable that this little European weed, so common on sandy or chalky lands in England, should be suspected in Queensland, where it has been introduced in course of cultivation and become naturalised, of causing such direful effect on stock in this colony, and is the more unaccountable when it is remembered that of the nearly 3,000 plants of the order to which it belongs none are known to possess secretions of a deleterious nature. In Queensland this plant is reported to affect horses much in the same way as vertigo or "staggers." Mr. J. Ivory, amongst others, supplies symptoms produced by it in the horse. After eating it the effect is best seen when the horse is at work. "All at once it stops, shivers all over, and if not allowed to spell a considerable time is almost sure to die. Cattle if only browsing and let alone are not affected by it. Bullocks when working very frequently die through the bad effects of the plant. Even if they do not die, they cannot work above two hours a day. When opened after death the stomachs have the appearance of having been burnt with strong acid."

Quantities of this weed are often brought into town mixed with the lucerne sold for greenstuff.

Dysphania myriocephala.

Order ILLECEBRACEÆ.

DYSPHANIA MYRIOCEPHALA,

Benth.; Flora Austr. v. 165.

A prostrate or procumbent glandularly hairy plant, often forming dense masses on land which is liable to floods, as around swamps. Leaves alternate, oblong, not much over $\frac{1}{4}$-inch long. The minute flowers in dense masses in the axils of the leaves. Abundant on damp land near Mantuan Downs; found in similar situations in all the Australian colonies.

A specimen of this plant was forwarded from the north-western portion of the Warrego district, where the drover in charge stated that he lost thirty rams out of a small flock, deaths taking place immediately after the first appearance of the symptoms; and that the thirty sheep all died within the space of a few minutes of each other. We have no other evidence to lead to the conclusion that this plant is poisonous.

Order THYMELÆACEÆ.

PIMELEA HÆMATOSTACHYA,

F. v. M., Fragm. i. 84; Flora Austr. vi. 22.

Plant erect, 1 or 2 feet high, of a grey colour, and but little branched; several inches of the upper portion is occupied by a dense spike of very showy flowers, varying in colour from a light-pink to a blood-red. Leaves opposite, oblong, 1 to nearly 2 inches long; when just beginning to flower, 4 to 8 linear, membranous, hairy leaves will be found close under the head of flowers, but these soon fall away. This plant is met with in many parts of North Queensland.

This is considered by many as one of our worst poison herbs, and is credited with killing hundreds of sheep. It is, however, stated that if the ears of a sheep poisoned by this herb are slit before the poison has taken much effect upon the animal its life may be saved.

The bark of the various species of this genus, and also *Wikstrœmia*, might be used by medical men when they require a substitute for the sometimes-used *Daphne mezereum*.—*Baron von Mueller in Melb. Chemist and Druggist.*

Pimelea pauciflora.

Order THYMELÆACEÆ.

PIMELEA PAUCIFLORA,

R. Br., Prod. 360; Flora Austr. vi. 27.

This plant often forms a dense bush of about 2 feet on open country, but on the borders of scrubs it often attains the height of 10 or more feet. Leaves narrow, over an inch long, opposite. Flowers only a very few in each head, of a greenish-yellow colour. Fruit reddish, small. This is found in Tasmania, Victoria, and New South Wales, as well as Queensland.

This plant has been suspected of poisoning sheep on the Darling Downs.

Order THYMELÆACEÆ.

PIMELEA SIMPLEX,

F. v. M. in Linnæa xxv. 443; Flora Austr. vi. 23.

This is an erect slender annual plant of about 1 foot in height, with alternate linear leaves about ¼-inch long; the flower-heads small, depressed-globular, surrounded when young by 2 to 4 involucral bracts, rather smaller but similar to the stem-leaves. Flowers small, covered by small hairs. This plant is met with in New South Wales, Victoria, South Australia, and southern Queensland.

This species is considered poisonous in New South Wales, where it is more abundant than in Queensland.

M. A. Hope. del. Gov.t Litho. Office Brisbane
Wikstroemia indica.

Order THYMELÆACEÆ.

WIKSTRŒMIA INDICA,

C. A. Mey. in Bull. Acad. Sc. Petersh. i. (1843) 357; Flora Austr. vi. 37; *Daphne indica*, Linn. in R. Br. Prod.; Hook. et Arn., Bot. Beech. t. 15.

A tall shrub or small tree, the young slender branches slightly silky-hairy. Leaves about 2 inches long, tapering towards each end. Flowers a few together at the ends of the branchlets, of a greenish-yellow colour, the tube nearly $\frac{1}{4}$-inch long. Fruit red, oval or oblong, about $\frac{1}{4}$-inch long. Abundant in Queensland from the margins of the rivers to the tops of the mountains; also in New South Wales, India, and China, with the islands of the Pacific.

This shrub is supposed to have poisoned stock who have browsed upon it in times of scarcity of feed.

Beyeria viscosa.

Order EUPHORBIACEÆ.

BEYERIA VISCOSA,

Miq. in Ann. Sc. Nat. ser. 3 i. 350 t. 15; Flora Austr. vi. 64; *Croton viscosum*, Labill., Pl. Nov. Holl. ii. 72 t. 222.

A tall shrub or small tree, the flowering and fruiting branches often viscid. Leaves oval-oblong, obtuse, tapering at the base to a short stalk; the upper surface somewhat smooth, the underside cottony-white, about 2 inches long. Some flowers male, others female, on stalks in the axils of the leaves; no petals, but the calyx-segments broad and coloured. Capsule ovoid-globular, 3-celled, 3-seeded. The plant is found in several parts of Queensland, New South Wales, Tasmania, and Western Australia.

We do not remember receiving this plant from any part of Queensland as a suspected poison shrub; but it is one of the poison shrubs of New South Wales, and has been there analysed and found to be so by the Government Analyst of New South Wales.

M.A. Hofsel, del.

Euphorbia Drummondii

Order EUPHORBIACEÆ.

EUPHORBIA DRUMMONDII,

Boiss., Cent. Euph. 14, and in DC. Prod. xvii. 36; Flora Austr. vi. 49.

Caustic Creeper.

A prostrate or diffuse, milky, much-branched plant, smooth, and of a light-grey colour, or here and there stained with red; the leaves oblong or nearly round, opposite on the stems, obtuse or notched at the end, about ¼-inch long. Flower-heads small, on short stalks, in the axils of the leaves. Capsule smooth, the seeds rough. This little plant is met with throughout Australia, including Tasmania.

An infusion of this herb is said by Mr. Wm. Shaw, of Tambo, writing to the *Queenslander*, May, 1879, to be useful in cases of chronic dysentery and low fever. Mr. Wm. Nepean Hutchison says the natives apply the milky sap to cuts and sores, which it possesses the power of quickly healing.

This weed is unquestionably poisonous to sheep; but, like our *Gastrolobium*, or Wallflower Poison-bush, seems to be comparatively, if not entirely, innocuous when in a dried state. It has been observed that, when eaten by sheep in the early morning before the heat of the sun has dried it up, it is almost certain to be fatal. It is seldom eaten to excess except by travelling sheep, and when grass is scarce. Its effect on sheep is curious. The head swells to an enormous extent, becoming so heavy that the animal cannot support it, and therefore drags it along the ground; the ears get much swollen and suppurate. In 1879 heavy losses occurred in a travelling flock, near Tambo, from this plant; and in 1882 an instance came under the personal observation of the Chief Inspector of Stock, where heavy losses occurred in the Dalby district, where the plant was growing in profusion at the time, in a flock of sheep travelling from the Warrego to the Darling Downs district. Mr. Wm. N. Hutchison says of the plant that it is a deadly poison to sheep, and that any part of the paunch of a sheep it touches is turned black or more of a putrid appearance, and that it takes but little to kill a sheep.

A specimen of this weed was lately sent to the *Queenslander* by Mr. J. T. Pope, from Augathella, for the purpose of obtaining its correct name, and in the accompanying letter the writer ascribes the further additional medicinal virtues to the plant :—"A friend of mine was suffering from inaction of the kidneys, water turbid, pains in back, etc. A lady here who had lived on a station gave her this weed to make into a tea; after drinking a pint, water plentiful and clear, and pains gone. The lady called the herb 'Old Clark,' from the name of the station-hand who first told her of its medicinal qualities."

In an interesting paper published in the *Australasian Medical Gazette* for October, 1886, Dr. Reid, of Port Germein, South Australia, gives details of a number of experiments made by him, which proved that in an alkaloid which he derived from this plant he has discovered a valuable new local anæsthetic which he used successfully in the cure of sciatica and in cases of sprain.

Order EUPHORBIACEÆ.

EUPHORBIA EREMOPHILA,

A. Cunn. in Mitch. Trop. Austr. 348; Boiss. in DC. Prod. xv. ii. 70, and Euph. Ic. t. 43; Flora Austr. vi. 52.

Saltern Creek Poison or Caustic plant.

Plant of stiff habit, erect, smooth, the divisions of the stem in pairs (dichotomous), 6 to 12 or more inches high, with a milky sap. The leaves on the lower part of the plant, and sometimes on the lateral branches, alternate; the others all opposite, stalked, linear, oblong, about 1 inch long, with distant teeth, leaving on the stem after falling off a gland-like scar. Flower-heads solitary in one axil of the pair of leaves; capsule smooth, about 2 lines long. Seeds rough, with a rather large caruncle (a protuberance at one end of the seed). Found throughout Australia.

This plant was suspected of causing the death of some sheep in a travelling flock of rams on Saltern Creek in July, 1886, but we have no direct evidence on the subject. It is, however, very probable, as the whole genus is more or less poisonous.

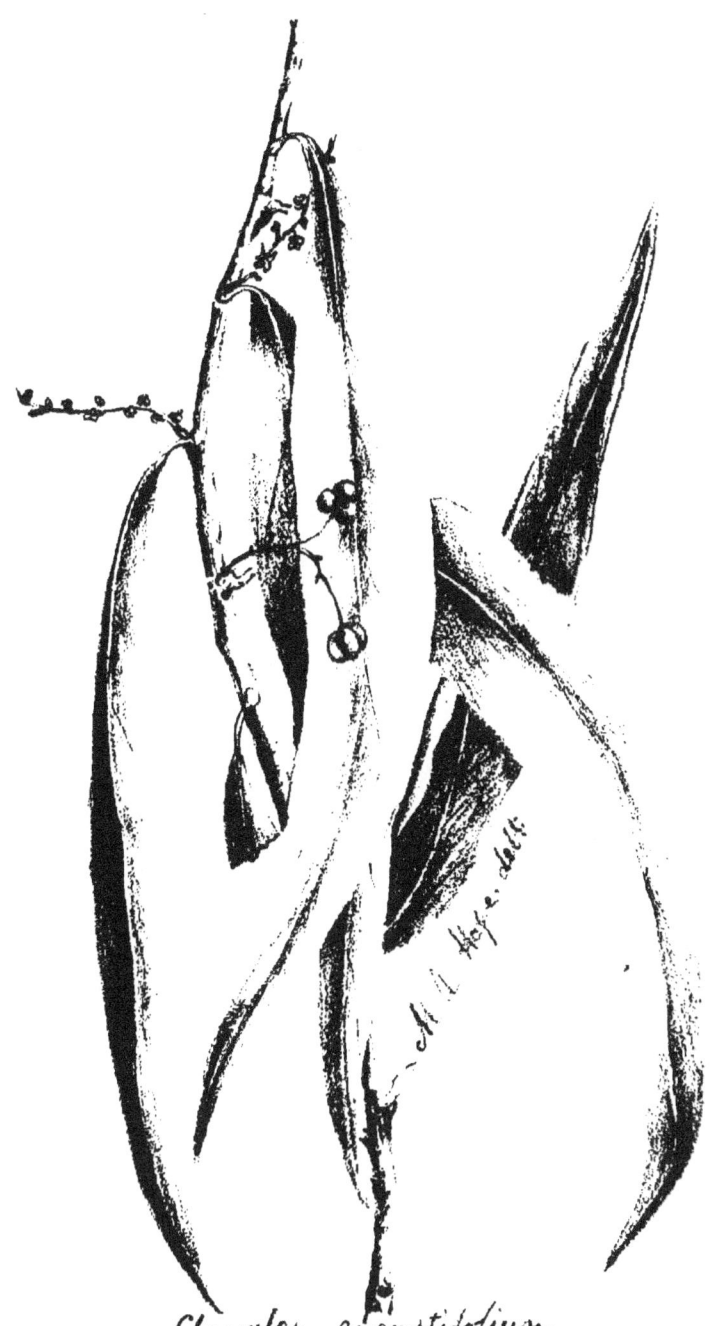

Claoxylon angustifolium.

Order EUPHORBIACEÆ.

CLAOXYLON ANGUSTIFOLIUM,

Muell. Arg. in Linnæa xxiv. 165, und in DC. Prod. xv. ii. 786; Flora Austr. vi. 129.

Bowen Poison-bush.

A tall shrub with narrow leaves 4 to 8 inches long, tapering towards each end and irregularly toothed; the footstalk sometimes ¼-inch long, at the top of which are very small glands. Flowers in slender racemes about 1 inch long; male and female flowers in the same cluster, but the latter on much longer stalks than the former; capsule smooth and grey, 3-lobed (tridymous), on a stalklet ½-inch long. Met with near Port Denison.

This was sent from near Bowen to Mr. K. T. Staiger in July, 1885, as a plant poisonous to stock.

Order EUPHORBIACEÆ.

RICINUS COMMUNIS,

Linn.; Roxb., Fl. Ind. iii. 689; Brandis 445; Kurz ii. 400; Gamble, Ind. Timbers 363; Bail., Syn. Queensl. Flora 480.

Castor Oil plant or *Palma Christi*.

A large shrub or small tree, the bark thin and usually of a light-brown. Wood light with a large central pith. Leaves often large, on long stalks, palmately divided into about 7 lance-shaped lobes, bearing saucer-shaped glands at the junction of the stalk and blade. Flowers in terminal panicles, the male flowers being produced on the lower portion and the female flowers on the upper portion of the inflorescence; the male flowers with numerous stamens, and the female flowers with forked, feathery, stigmatic branches to the styles. Fruit covered by soft prickles, 3-celled, 3-seeded. Seeds mottled, and a small sponge-like excrescence at one end. Indigenous in Arabia and North Africa, but become naturalised throughout India, as it seems to be doing in the warmer parts of Australia.

It has often been asserted that this plant is poisonous to stock. Mr. J. Harward de Rinzy, whilst giving evidence before the Royal Commission on Vegetable Products, Victoria, is reported ("Third Progress Report," p. 21) to have stated that the seed is "a deadly poison," and that he had lost one of his best horses from its having eaten of them. This assertion is somewhat qualified and explained by him when speaking in reference to the oil, when he remarks: "If cold drawn it is suited for medicinal purposes; but if hot drawn it is poisonous, and the eating of two or three of the dry and pleasant-flavoured seeds is deadly, inducing Asiatic cholera."—*L.c.*

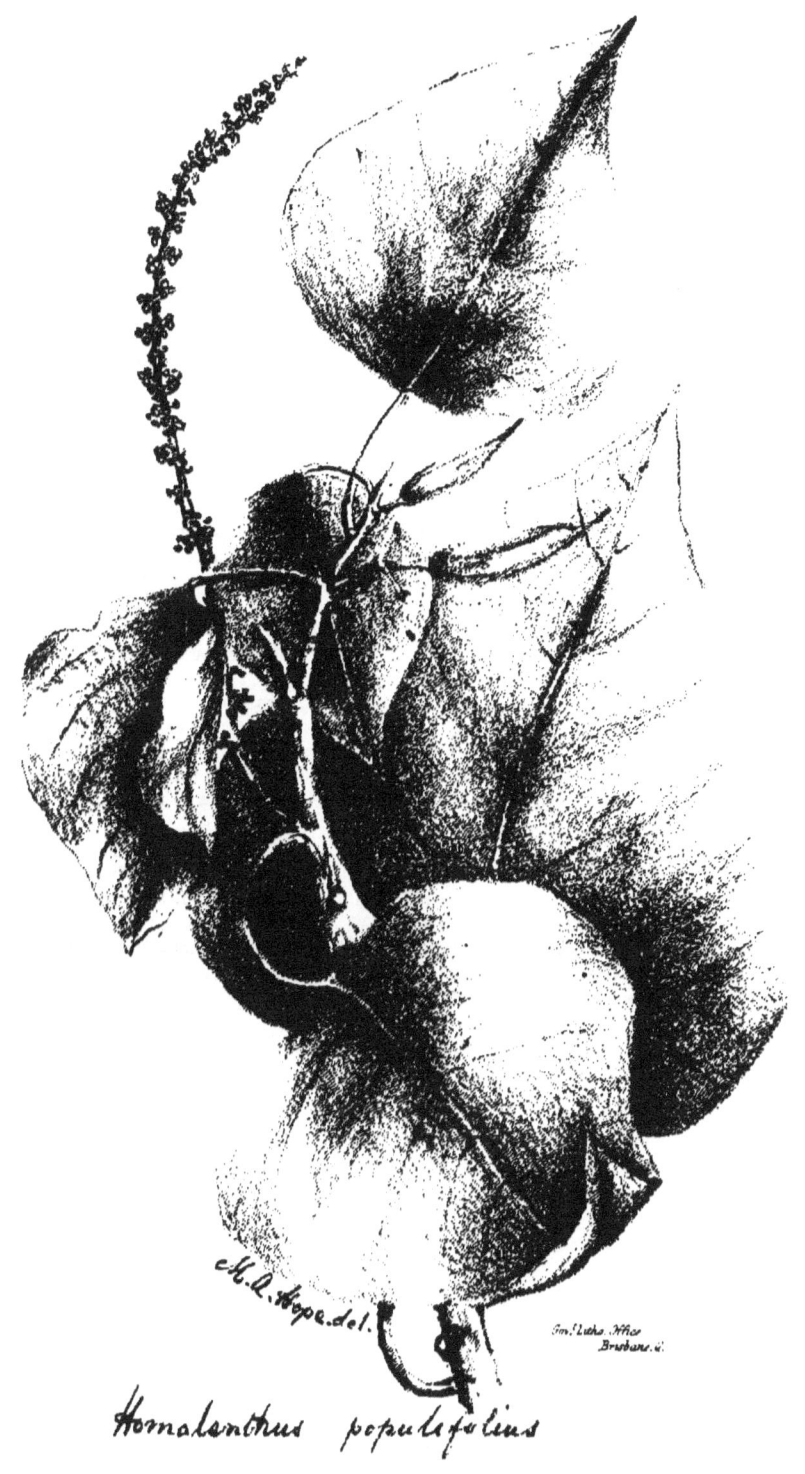

Homalanthus populifolius

Order EUPHORBIACEÆ.

HOMALANTHUS POPULIFOLIUS,

Grah. in Bot. Mag. t. 2780; F. v. M., Fragm. i. 32; *Carumbium populifolium*, Reinw. in Flora Austr. vi. 150.

Bulli Poison-bush.

A quite smooth tall shrub or small tree, of a greyish-blue colour, the fading leaves often turning a reddish-purple. Leaves like those of the Poplar, from 2 to 6 inches long and nearly as broad, on long stalks. The stipules (leaf-like appendages on the stem at the insertion of the leaf-stalk) about 1 inch long, but very deciduous (soon falling away). Flowers in racemes about 3 or 4 inches long. Bracts (the small leaves attending the flowers) small-toothed, with 2 large glands at their base. The female flowers at the base of the raceme; capsule bluish-grey, didymous (two together), from $\frac{1}{4}$ to $\frac{1}{2}$ inch across. Seeds with a rather large fleshy carunculus or protuberance.

This is a plant enjoying a very wide range; scarcely any of the Queensland scrubs are without it. It is also common in New South Wales, reaching into Gippsland, Victoria, all over the Eastern Archipelago, and some of the islands of the Pacific, Ceylon, and other parts of the globe.

Baron von Mueller, the Government Botanist of Victoria, writing to the "Australasian Chemist and Druggist," September, 1883, says that "cattle, when extensively browsing on the foliage, are apt to succumb to its effects; the final cause of death being *hæmaturia*." He also says that Mr. W. Kirton, of Bulli, near Illawarra, informed him that "large losses of cattle had occurred from their eating this shrub in seasons of scarcity of feed."

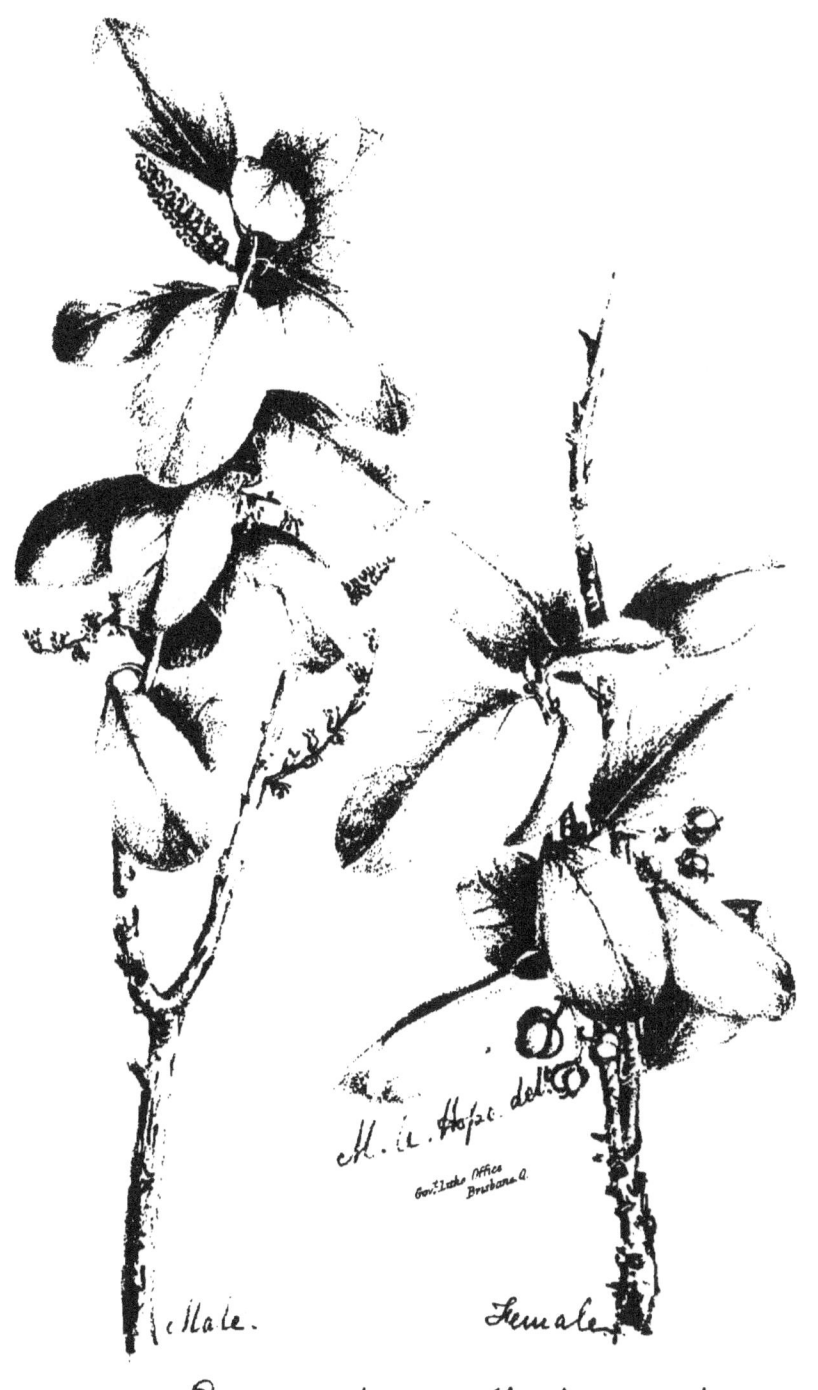

Order EUPHORBIACEÆ.

EXCÆCARIA AGALLOCHA,

Linn.; Muell. Arg. in DC. Prod. xv. ii. 1220; Flora Austr. vi. 152.

The Milky Mangrove or River Poison tree.

This is usually a small tree of crooked growth, and met with on the borders of tidal rivers and coast swamps in Queensland, Tropical Asia, &c. The sap is milky and highly poisonous; the leaves, which are alternate on the branches, are rather thick, obovate, and of a yellowish-green colour. The male flowers are borne in rather dense spikes of 2 to 3 inches in length, of a reddish colour; the female flowers in much shorter spikes and pale green. Capsules tridymous (growing in threes). Seeds globular without carunculus.

In India the sap of this tree is known as "tiger's milk," and applied to inveterate ulcers with good effect. Cattle seldom browse on the foliage, yet when in times of scarcity they have eaten it it has been suspected of causing their death. Some years ago one of Mr. J. G. Cribb's children was nearly killed by sucking the milk of this tree by mistake for fig-tree sap; he soon became very ill, and lying down on the grass by the roadside would likely have died from the effects of the poison had he not been found by a person passing, by whom he was recognised and carried home, where a powerful emetic was administered and medical assistance at once sent for.

Male. Female.
Excoecaria Dallachyana.

Order EUPHORBIACEÆ.

EXCÆCARIA DALLACHYANA,

Baill., Adans. vi. 324 ; Flora Austr. vi. 153.

Scrub Poison-tree.

A small slender scrub tree met with in most Queensland scrubs, both north and south, and known as Scrub Poison-tree on account of the poisonous nature of its milky sap. Leaves dark-green, rather thick, 1 to 3 inches long, narrow-ovate, bordered by blunt teeth. Flowers in short spikes. Capsules tridymous (3-lobed or growing in threes).

Now and again samples of this have been sent in as a scrub poison.

Trema aspera.

Order URTICACEÆ.

TREMA ASPERA,

Blume, Mus. Bot. ii. 58; Flora Austr. vi. 158.

Generally known in Queensland as the Peach-leaf Poison-bush.

A tall erect shrub or slender tree; the branches and leaves rough, with short rigid hairs. Leaves narrow-ovate, broad at the base, and tapering much towards the point, with three longitudinal ribs, hairy and rough to the touch. The flowers, which are very small, are borne in clusters in the axils of the leaves, and are succeeded by small black berries. The shrub is very abundant throughout Queensland, reaching into New South Wales.

In dry seasons and in dry localities this bush is pretty generally considered to be poisonous to stock, while in other parts where the feed is more succulent nothing is heard of its having any ill effects. Some stock-owners are said to have tested its effects upon stock by confining a few in a yard and giving them nothing but this shrub to eat, when it is stated to have killed them. We are inclined to think that the stock must have died from indigestion, for it could hardly be expected that they could long subsist on such tough fibrous matter as shoots of this bush.

Order URTICACEÆ.

TREMA AMBOINENSIS,
Blume, Mus. Bot. ii. 61 ; Flora Austr. vi. 159.

A tall shrub or small tree, the branchlets densely hairy, with short more or less velvety hairs. Leaves ovate, somewhat like the Peach-leaf Poison-bush, but more velvety, on shorter stalks, and with more prominent veins than that species The flower-cymes are also more compact and shorter—differences, however, often overlooked by the bushman. This shrub is not met with out of the tropics in Australia, while *T. aspera* reaches into New South Wales. It, however, is common in East India and the Archipelago, and also South China.

Mr. James Lamond, of Carl Creek, writing to the Chief Inspector of Stock, says :—"I know this shrub to be poisonous in the North, having lost working bullocks who had eaten it during times of drought."

NOTE.—Baron von Mueller, in "Census of Australian Plants," includes all the Australian *Tremas* under *T. cannabina*, Loureiro.

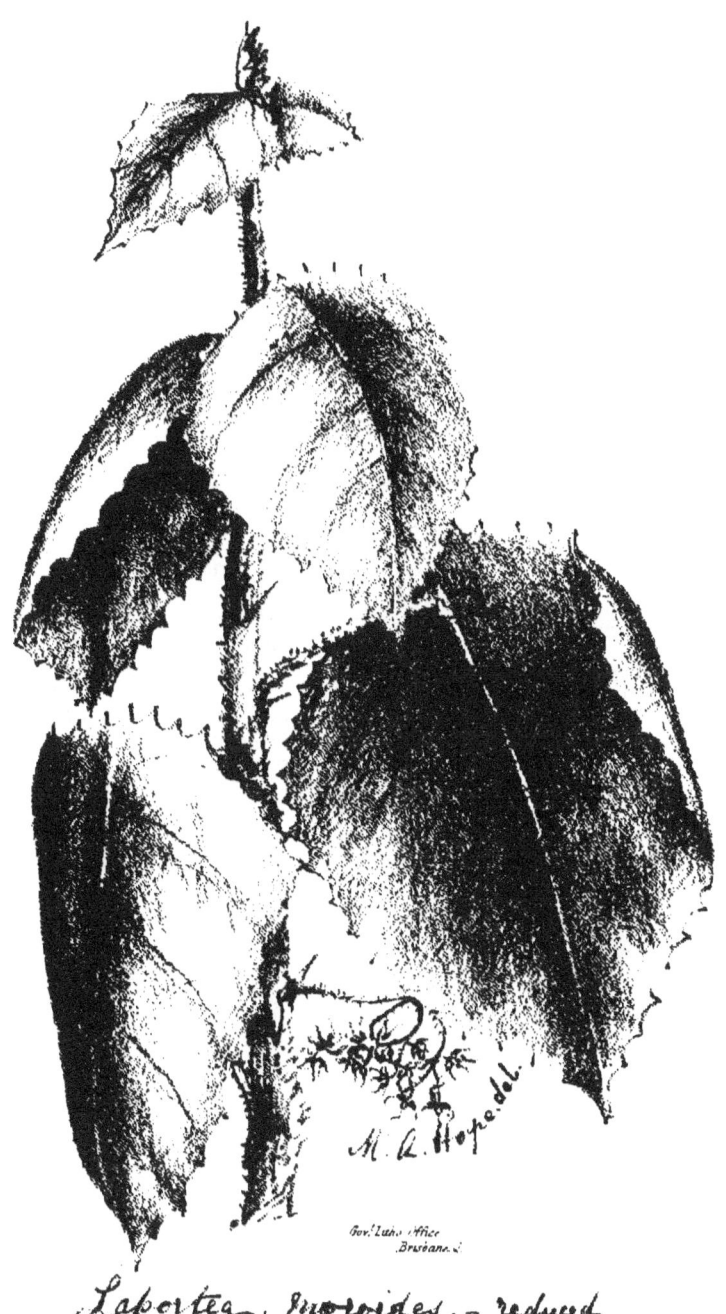

Laportea moroides. - reduced

Order URTICACEÆ.

LAPORTEA MOROIDES,

Wedd. Monogr. Urt. 142, and DC. Prod. vii. i. 88.

The native name of this stinging tree is "Gympie."

It is a tall shrub or small tree, a most virulent stinger, found too abundant in some scrubs both north and south. The leaves are often very large and have a soft appearance, are placed peltately on their stalks (that is, the blade or expanded part of the leaf is attached to its stalk some distance in from the margin), and on the upper surface a red spot usually marks the place where the leaf is attached to the stalk. Bunches of crinkly, purplish, fleshy fruit usually on the stem of the branches below the leaves or in the axils of the lower leaves.

This perhaps should hardly be placed amongst the poisonous plants of the colony, but the virulent effect of its stinging hairs have in Northern Queensland frequently caused the death of horses.

Crinum angustifolium

Order AMARYLLIDEÆ.

CRINUM ANGUSTIFOLIUM,

R. Br., Prod. 297; *C. asiaticum*, var. *angustifolium*, Benth., Flora Austr. vi. 455; *C. arenarium*, Herb. Bot. Mag. t. 2355; *C. australasicum*, var. *arenarium*, Herb. Amaryll. 259; Kunth, Enum. v. 567; Gard. Chron. 1881.

Bulb subglobose with a very short neck. Leaves linear, $1\frac{1}{2}$ to 2 feet long, 1 to $1\frac{1}{2}$ inches broad, of firm texture; veins close, tapering gradually towards the point; margins rough or with distant small sharp teeth. Scape or stalk bearing the flowers somewhat over 1 foot high, bearing an umbel of usually 5 flowers. Flowers on short stalklets. The spath-valves or bracts under the umbel lanceolate, 2 or more inches long. Flower-tube slender, 3 or 4 inches long, the spreading segments lanceolate, 2 to 3 inches long and about $\frac{1}{3}$-inch broad at the middle. Filaments red, shorter than segments of flower, bearing anthers of about $\frac{1}{2}$-inch in length. Style long.—*Gard. Chron., l.c.* The Queensland plant has broader leaves, and often 10 to 12 flowers in the umbel.

This is the *Crinum* often met with on sandy lands and downs, and suspected of deleterious properties.

Order AMARYLLIDEÆ.

CRINUM PEDUNCULATUM,

R. Br., Prod. 297; Flora Austr. vi. 455.

The River or Swamp White Lily of Queensland and New South Wales.

This is a much larger plant than *C. angustifolium*, with broader leaves, whose edges are smooth, often with a stout stem 1 or 2 feet high; the leaves strap-like, 2 to 4 inches broad. Flower-stem 3 or 4 feet high, bearing a large umbel of showy white fragrant flowers; each flower in the umbel on a rather long pedicel; segments of flower long, strap-like; capsules bearing a few large, globular, bluntly angular seeds.

Plants of this species are rather numerous in some of our swamps, and have been thought to have poisoned stock, who crop them closely down during long droughts.

Hope delt. Bulbine bulbosa.

ORDER LILIACEÆ.

BULBINE BULBOSA,

Haw., Rev. Pl. Succ. 33; Flora Austr. vii. 35; *Anthericum bulbosum*, R. Br. Prod. 275; Bot. Mag. t. 3017.

Native Onion or Leek.

Leaves and flower-stalk arising from a bulb-like rootstock. Leaves somewhat like those of an Onion, only deep-green, 6 to 12 inches long. Flower-stalk bearing in its upper half numerous yellow flowers about 1 inch in diameter; the stamens about of equal length, with a tuft of hairs on each just below the anther, or half the filament clothed with hairs; capsule erect, about ¼-inch diameter, containing 1 or 2 seeds. Found in Tasmania and perhaps throughout Australia, with the exception of Western Australia.

Specimens of this plant were sent from the neighbourhood of Aramac, where it was reported to have caused the death of a number of travelling rams in charge of Edward Bright, in July, 1886.

Mr. Wm. Nepean Hutchison, Sheep Inspector, Warrego, says of this Native Leek:—"Its effects on cattle, sheep, and horses are almost the same—continually lying down, rolling, terribly scoured, mucous discharge from the nose of a green and yellowish colour. Cattle survive the longest; sheep take some three days, and horses will linger for a week. To a pony of mine poisoned by this weed I gave 10 drops of laudanum in half-a-bottle of castor oil three times during the day; also applied three bran poultices on the loins. This appeared to give immediate relief, as previously he could hardly use his hind legs, and was lying down with his head towards his sides biting his flanks. His urine was thick and green till after the second dose, when it appeared in its natural state; his eye sunken and flanks shaking."

Bulbine semibarbata

ORDER LILIACEÆ.

BULBINE SEMIBARBATA,

Haw., Rev. Pl. Succ. 33; Flora Austr. vii. 35; *Anthericum semibarbatum*, R. Br Prod. 275, but not *A. semibarbatum*, Hook. Bot. Mag. t. 3129.

The Lesser Leek or Onion.

Root fibrous. Leaves and flowers much smaller than in *B. bulbosa*, and only 3 of the stamens bearded, and these longer than the others. Capsule ripening 3 or 4 angular black seeds.

Met with throughout Australia and Tasmania, usually on sandy wet land. Effect on stock the same as *B. bulbosa*, and known under the same local name by stockmen.

Order AROIDEÆ.

COLOCASIA MACRORRHIZA,

Schott., Meletem. 18; Flora Austr. vii. 155.

Arum or Cunjevoi.

Stem often of old plants from 3 to 6 feet high. Leaves broadly heart-shaped, on stalks of 1 to 3 feet with sheathing bases. Flowers yellowish, fragrant, about 4 to 6 inches long but narrow, succeeded by a bunch of red fleshy berries.

It has been thought at times that this plant has caused the death of cattle grazing on scrub lands, but we know of no authenticated case.

The acrid milky juice from the base of the stems of this plant gives instant relief from the pain caused by the sting of the Nettle-trees.

In concluding this enumeration of the suspected or reputed poison plants of Queensland we would briefly draw attention to a few Fungi, which certainly are injurious to fodders as lessening their nutritive qualities, and probably may in some cases be poisonous to stock feeding upon the infected plants. It may be an open question as to whether the Fungi here brought under notice, and similar forms, are such as may be termed poisonous; yet it has been noticed in Europe that during those years in which cattle have suffered most from disease the "red rust" and "mildew" have also been most prevalent.

PUCCINIA GRAMINIS,
Pers., Disp. Fung. 39.

Trichobasis rubigo-vera, *Uredo rubigo*, and *U. linearis* are only forms of this plant—the Corn Mildew and Red Rust. It is commonly to be met with on a wiry, harsh grass called *Hemarthria compressa*, found usually around swamps and on low-lying land, and at the present time abundant on *Andropogon intermedius*, in Albert Park.

USTILAGO AXICOLA,
Berk., Ann. Nat. Hist. (1852) No. 55.

On low, damp, undrained soil this fungus is generally to be met with in great abundance on the inflorescence of a little Sedge (*Fimbristylis diphylla*).

USTILAGO CARBO,
Tul. Mem. Ustil. 78 (*U. segetum*, Ditm.).

The Standing Corn Smut.

This fungus affects badly a species of *Aristida*, the three-awned Spear-grass in the Western districts.

THECAPHORA GLOBULIFERA,
Berk. and Broome, Trans. Linn. Soc. i. 407.

Rice-grass Fungus.

This is a somewhat globular fungus which attacks the panicles of the Rice-grass (*Leersia hexandra*, Sw.). Sometimes it is very abundant, and it is probable when rice is more generally grown that this pest will be destructive to that grain.

TILLETIA EPIPHYLLA,
Berk. and Broome in Trans. Linn. Soc. ii. 67.

Maize Rust.

Dr. Bancroft found the maize badly affected with this rust on several farms in 1878, and from the specimens collected then by him the species was characterised.

SPHÆRELLA DESTRUCTIVA,

Berk. et Broome in Trans. Linn. Soc. ii. 71, t. 15, f. 22-24.

The Lucerne Fungus.

This fungus may be seen very thick on much of the lucerne which is now being brought into town for green fodder. It is a comparatively new species, being described from specimens found by one of the writers on a patch of lucerne growing at a farm near Indooroopilly, about 1879. It, as in the case of other plant-parasites, seems to attack the lucerne mostly on spots badly drained, or where the plants from age and continual cutting have become weak. Judging from samples brought into town, the crops of lucerne must be suffering much from this pest, and if fodder thus affected is not really poisonous to the animals eating it, the nutritive qualities of such fodder must necessarily be much less than that free from this fungus.

GLŒOSPORIUM CUCURBITARUM,

Berk. and Broome in Trans. Linn. Soc. ii. 68.

Melon Fungus.

This is a fungus which attacks the fruit of the water-melon, but its ill effects are most felt when it preys upon the fruit of kinds kept for winter food for stock, as it soon renders them a rotten mass.

CLADOSPORIUM HERBARUM,

Link., Obs. ii. 37.

This, a common fungus found on many substances, often may be noticed covering the inflorescence of *Ischæmum triticeum* and *Paspalum scrobiculatum*, two grasses often found on low damp soil. It forms a soft, dense, olive-black substance.

HELMINTHOSPORIUM RAVENELII,

Curtis. in Sill. Journ. (1848) 352.

This fungus is known in America as "Blackseed," and is said to attack the "Rattail Grass" (*Sporobolus indicus*). This grass, as well as other species of the same genus, is also often affected with it in Queensland, especially on low damp land. This black mould often occupies the whole of the inflorescence.

If the few following be added to the foregoing suspected poison plants, this pamphlet may be said to record all those—both indigenous and naturalised—which are obnoxious to Queensland pastoralists.

ACÆNA OVINA, A. Cunn.
ACÆNA SANGUISORBÆ, Vahl.

These plants have burr-like dry fruits, annoying to the sheep-farmer by their becoming entangled in the wool. They are only found in the southern parts of this colony, but in the southern colonies and in New Zealand they are much more abundant and troublesome.

CNICUS LANCEOLATUS, Linn.

The Scotch Thistle of Queensland.

A too well known troublesome plant, hard to eradicate when once established on good soil.

CENTAUREA MELITENSIS, Linn.

At some places called "Star Thistle."

This is a roadside obnoxious weed now spreading over our downs country.

MARTYNIA FRAGRANS, Lindl.

The fruit of this showy flowering plant is a dry, hard, rough capsule with two long, terminal, curved, sharp, hooked horns which attach to the wool of a passing sheep and tear it off in handfuls. Fortunately the plant is as yet not very widely spread.

The following grasses when in seed are more or less injurious [to wool-growing :—

HETEROPOGON CONTORTUS, Rœm. and Schultz.

The Bunch Spear-grass.

When in seed the panicles of this grass catch together and form large masses of a brown colour; the sharp spear-like seeds are very injurious to sheep, but the grass produces a fair fodder for cattle.

HETEROPOGON INSIGNIS, Thw.

The Tall Spear-grass of the tropical coast lands. This grass often attains a height of 10 to 12 feet.

STIPA SEMIBARBATA, R. Br.
STIPA PUBESCENS, R. Br.
STIPA SETACEA, R. Br.
STIPA ARISTIGLUMUS, F. v. M.

Are all known as Spear-grasses, and are excellent fodders before the seed ripens, but become then more or less troublesome.

The same may be said of *Aristida*, a genus of grasses known at once from *Stipa* by its awns being not single but in threes. The species of this genus are by no means bad pasture grasses, although troublesome at the time the seed is ripening.

www.ingramcontent.com/pod-product-compliance
Lightning Source LLC
Chambersburg PA
CBHW020134170426
43199CB00010B/740